FLOOD!

The 1993 Midwest Downpours

by Barbara Knox

Consultant: Daniel H. Franck, Ph.D.

BEARPORT
PUBLISHING COMPANY, INC.

New York, New York

Credits

Cover, Background, Richard Hamilton Smith/CORBIS; Front(main), AP / Wide World Photos; (inset), Fritz Hoffman/Image Works/Image Works/Time Life Pictures/Getty Images; Back, Don Emmert / AFP / Getty Images; Title page, Fritz Hoffman/Image Works/Image Works/Time Life Pictures/Getty Images; Page 4, Charles Palek / Animals Animals - Earth Scenes; 5, 6, Najlah Feanny / CORBIS; 8, 9, Andrea Booher / FEMA Photo; 10, Richard Hamilton Smith/CORBIS; 11, Andrea Booher / FEMA Photo; 12, AP / Wide World Photos; 13, Stock Connection / PictureQuest; 14, 15, Library of Congress Prints & Photographs Division; 16, Reuters / CORBIS; 17, Andrea Booher / FEMA Photo; 18, Eugene Garcia / AFP / Getty Images; 19, Getty Images; 20, David Muench / CORBIS; 21, Tom & Pat Leeson / Ardea; 22, Richard Day / Daybreak Imagery; 23, John Zich / Time Life Pictures / Getty Images; 24, AP / Wide World Photos; 25, courtesy of www.waterstructures.com / AquaDam; 26, Doug DuKane; 27, Richard Cummins / CORBIS; 29, Andrea Booher/FEMA Photo.

Design and production by Dawn Beard Creative, Triesta Hall of Blu-Design, and Octavo Design and Production, Inc.

Library of Congress Cataloging-in-Publication Data

Knox, Barbara.
  Flood! : the 1993 midwest downpours / by Barbara Knox.
     p. cm. — (X-treme disasters that changed America)
  Includes bibliographical references and index.
  ISBN 1-59716-172-1 (lib. bdg.) — ISBN 1-59716-198-5 (pbk.)
  1. Floods—Middle West—Juvenile literature. 2. Emergency management—
Middle West—Juvenile literature. I. Title. II. Series.

  GB1399.4.M6K66 2006
  977'.033—dc22
                                            2005026079

For more information, write to Bearport Publishing Company, Inc., 101 Fifth Avenue, Suite 6R, New York, New York 10003. Printed in the United States of America.

1 2 3 4 5 6 7 8 9 10

Table of Contents

Rising Water 4

Midwest Under Water 6

Shut Down. 8

How Does a Flood Start? .10

The Nature of Floods 12

A Killer Flash Flood. 14

Fighting Floods. 16

After the Flood 18

A Rising Problem. 20

Time for Change 22

New Tools for the Fight 24

Learning to Live with the River 26

Just the Facts 28

Glossary 30

Bibliography 31

Read More. 31

Learn More Online 31

Index 32

About the Author 32

Rising Water

Eight-year-old Dustin was scared. He sat in his dad's truck with his sister Dana. Wide-eyed, he watched as rising water leaked into the **cab**. Outside, water covered their yard and part of their house.

▲ The Missouri River floods the town of Hartsburg, Missouri, in 1993.

Dustin's dad, Steve, jumped into the truck. He tried to back down the driveway. The truck wouldn't move! The racing water was pushing against the truck, holding it in place. Faster and faster, the water kept rising. Finally, the truck roared backward.

Quickly, Steve drove his family to a **shelter** on dry ground. There, they would be safe while the raging river flooded the land.

▲ A home under water in West Alton, Illinois

Dustin and his family lived in Halstead, Kansas. The flood swept through their town on July 15, 1993.

Midwest Under Water

The Great Midwest **Flood** of 1993 ruined Dustin's home that day. Rushing water swept away his clothes and his baseball card collection. Even his bed was gone.

▲ High floodwaters in an Illinois neighborhood

Dustin was not the only child to lose his home. The killer flood roared through nine states. Dirty water poured into hundreds of big cities. Seventy-five small towns were completely destroyed.

The flood continued from April through September. When it was over, 48 people were dead and more than 60,000 homes were wrecked. The flood caused $15 billion worth of damage.

The 1993 flood affected North Dakota, South Dakota, Minnesota, Wisconsin, Iowa, Nebraska, Kansas, Missouri, and Illinois.

Shut Down

When the flood spread across the land, the water destroyed bridges, roads, and farms. Ten airports shut down. **Barge** traffic in the rivers stopped for two months. For weeks, no trains ran through the Midwest.

When the flood ruined bridges, people had to cross the rivers on ferryboats. Florida sent ferryboats up to the Midwest to help.

In Des Moines, Iowa, dirty floodwater poured into the city's water supply. Suddenly, 250,000 people didn't have water. No one could flush a toilet or take a shower. There was no water to drink. Trucks from other states brought bottled water to the people. It took almost two weeks to fix the problem. Even then, people had to boil the tap water to make it safe for drinking.

▲ People in Iowa receiving clean water

How Does a Flood Start?

The 1993 flood began slowly. In the spring, snow had melted and soaked into the ground. Some of the melting snow ran into rivers, which wasn't a problem, until rain began to fall.

▲ Heavy storm clouds in Minnesota

Usually, rain is measured in inches. In the summer of 1993, however, some parts of the Midwest got more than four *feet* (1 m) of rain. Where did all that water go?

The ground soaks up water like a sponge. When the ground is **saturated**, the water spreads across the surface. It pours into streams and rivers. Then the rivers begin to rise and overflow their **banks**.

▲ An aerial view of the overflowing Mississippi River

In 1993, both the **Mississippi River** and the **Missouri River** overflowed. They are the two largest rivers in the United States.

The Nature of Floods

Floods are the most common natural disaster in the United States. Every year, they kill about 140 people and cause about $4 billion worth of damage.

▲ Two dams burst and sent water rushing downriver in Michigan in 2003.

Ninety-five percent of people killed in **flash floods** are trying to outrun the water. To avoid the water, it is best to climb up hills and rocks.

All floods, though, are not alike. Flash floods occur when a **dam** bursts or heavy rain falls in a short time. They can develop in minutes. With no warning, people can be trapped in the rising water. Flash floods kill more people than any other type of flood.

The one in 1993 was due to many rivers flooding at the same time. **Levees** broke and the water rushed out of the rivers and over the land.

◄ The Mississippi River breaks through a levee during flooding.

A Killer Flash Flood

One of the deadliest floods in U.S. history happened in Johnstown, Pennsylvania. On a cold, rainy day in May 1889, a dam burst on a lake high in the mountains. Twenty million tons (18 million metric tons) of water exploded through the broken dam. The icy water roared down through the valley. The wall of water reached 60 feet (18 m) high.

▲ Main Street after the flood

Fourteen miles (23 km) downriver, people in Johnstown heard a loud boom. Minutes later, the wave swept through the town. When it was over, more than 2,200 people were dead. Many more were missing and never seen again.

▲ The Johnstown flood caused $17 million worth of damage.

Water rushed from the broken dam at 40 miles per hour (64 kph). Cars on city streets travel at 20 to 30 miles per hour (32 to 48 kph).

Fighting Floods

In the 1920s, the government began fighting floods. They built hundreds of levees along major rivers. Usually, the levees held the water back. In the 1993 flood, however, the levees were not tall enough.

▼ People help block a flooding river in Illinois.

Thousands of **volunteers** came to the Midwest to fight the flood. They filled bags with sand. Then they piled the sandbags on top of the levees. Sometimes the wall of sandbags held the river back. Often, though, the river broke through.

People also piled sandbags around their homes to keep the water out. Townspeople worked together to save stores, churches, and schools.

One truckload of sand fills about 2,000 sandbags. In the 1993 flood, people filled more than 26.5 million sandbags.

After the Flood

When the water finally went down, the Midwest was covered in mud. Dead fish, garbage, and ruined buildings lay everywhere. It was time to clean up.

Homeowners used shovels to clear mud out of living rooms and kitchens. They hauled filthy rugs and furniture outside. They scrubbed slimy walls, floors, and ceilings with bleach.

Floodwater that has soaked into household items makes it easier for bacteria to grow. Bleach kills bacteria, which can cause disease.

▲ Flood victims throw out their damaged couch.

As they cleaned, they found that animals, such as snakes, toads, and worms, had moved inside their homes. Everywhere people went, the smell of rotting fish and wet wood cut through the air. For many people, the cleanup was the worst part of the flood. Others, however, had nothing left to clean up.

▲ Homeowners clean out their flooded home.

A Rising Problem

Rivers have been overflowing for thousands of years. The water used to spread into **wetlands** alongside the river where only plants, animals, and birds lived.

▼ Wetlands in Missouri

However, after the government started building levees, people began moving closer to the rivers. They thought they would be safe from floods. They built towns and farms. Soon thousands of people lived alongside the mighty rivers.

However, during a flood, living along the rivers caused many problems. When water broke through the levees, all the nearby towns were flooded. Farmers lost their land. Rushing water swept away animals, homes, and cars.

The wetlands are home to many different types of birds such as ducks, geese, and herons.

Time for Change

After the 1993 flood, the government decided to make some changes. It used to help people rebuild their homes or businesses after a flood. Now, the government would buy the land instead. It would help people move out of the **floodplains**.

▲ A flooded farm in Valmeyer, Illinois

More than 10,000 families and businesses have moved away from the Mississippi and Missouri rivers. The government even moved one whole town. It helped the people of Valmeyer, Illinois, move their town to higher ground.

Now, when Midwest rivers flood, fewer people are in the way. Water can spill out into the floodplains. The water renews the wetlands and creates a home for wildlife.

▲ Mayor Dennis Knobloch helps break ground in a field that will be the site for the new town of Valmeyer.

In Missouri, 50,000 acres (20,234 hectares) of floodplains have been turned back into wetlands.

New Tools for the Fight

Today people have better ways to fight back against floods. Instead of sandbags, which are heavy and take time to fill, people can use flood **barriers**. These metal and plastic sheets can be hooked together. Just a few people can quickly build a long wall. The wall holds back the water.

▲ A flood barrier being constructed.

There is also another type of flood barrier that looks like a big hose. People lay the long tube on the ground near their home. Then they fill it with water. Floodwaters can't get past the tube.

▲ A house being protected by a flood control tube.

The 1993 flood was called a "100 Year Flood." Floods that huge only happen about once every 100 years.

Learning to Live with the River

Floods can be deadly, but there are lots of things that people can do to stay safe. Every family living in a flood area should keep a disaster kit on hand. The kit should include canned food, bottled water, batteries, a change of clothes, and first-aid supplies. Since a flood can knock out the electricity, it's also important to have a battery-powered radio to get information.

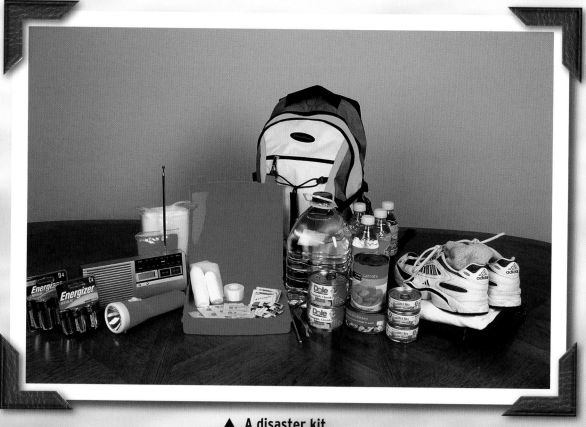

▲ A disaster kit

We can't stop floods from happening. However, everyone has the knowledge to be ready. Everyone can be prepared for a flood.

▲ St. Louis, Missouri today

If told to leave your home or school during a flood, you should do so as soon as possible.

Just the Facts

The 1993 Midwest Flood

- On July 13, two inches (5 cm) of rain fell in Des Moines, Iowa, in just 20 minutes. The force of the water **runoff** caused manhole covers to pop open.
- The flood covered an area 500 miles (805 km) long and 200 miles (322 km) wide.
- The town of Grafton, Illinois, was under water for 195 days.

The power of floods

- Rushing water just six inches (15 cm) deep can knock a grown man off his feet.
- A car or bus will float in water that is two feet (1 m) deep.
- Flash floods can rip trees from the ground and move huge boulders.
- River floods have been known to sweep away two-story buildings.

Other deadly floods

- The worst flood in United States history happened in Galveston, Texas. In 1900, a powerful hurricane struck the city. A wall of water 16 feet (5 m) high swept over the land. More than 8,000 people died.
- Floods in other parts of the world have been much worse. In 1931, the Yellow River in China flooded. Almost four million people died.

- Flash floods move so quickly that sometimes people cannot get to safety in time. In 1972, a flash flood near Rapid City, South Dakota, killed 238 people within a few hours.
- In summer 2005, a hurricane sent water crashing into New Orleans, Louisiana. Levees broke and the entire city was under water. More than 100,000 people lost their homes in one day. Over 1,000 people were killed.

Changes in America caused by floods

- Levees are being built taller to keep rivers from flooding.
- People are using flood barriers to protect their homes and businesses.
- With the government's help, people are moving away from floodplains.

▲ Animals as well as people had to be rescued during the 1993 flood.

29

Glossary

banks (BANGKS)   the land along both sides of a river

barge (BARJ)   a flat-bottomed boat used to carry goods on the river

barriers (BA-ree-urz)   things that block the way

cab (KAB)   the front part of a truck, where people sit

dam (DAM)   a solid wall built to hold back water

flash floods (FLASH FLUHDZ)   floods that happen quickly

flood (FLUHD)   a huge flow of water that spreads over land

floodplains (FLUHD-planez)   flat lands on each side of a river where water naturally overflows during a flood

levees (LEV-eez)   high walls of dirt and rocks built alongside a river to stop flooding

Mississippi River (MIH-sih-*sip*-pee RIV-ur)   a major river in the United States; flows from Minnesota to Louisiana

Missouri River (mih-ZUR-ee RIV-ur)   the longest river in the United States; flows from Montana into the Mississippi River in the state of Missouri

runoff (RUHN-awf)   water flowing off the land

saturated (SACH-uh-*ray*-tid)   soaked completely so that no more liquid can be taken in

shelter (SHEL-tur)   a safe place that covers or protects people or animals

volunteers (*vol*-uhn-TIHRZ)   people who help others for free

wetlands (WET-landz)   swampy areas near lakes and rivers

Bibliography

Amato, Joseph, and Janet Timmerman, eds. *At the Headwaters: The 1993 Flood in Southwestern Minnesota.* Marshall, MN: MN Conservation Corps/ Southwest State University Flood Recovery Project (1995).

Kahl, Jonathan. *National Audubon Society First Field Guide: Weather.* New York: Scholastic (1998).

Lauber, Patricia. *Flood: Wrestling with the Mississippi.* Washington, D.C.: National Geographic Society (1996).

Vogel, Carole G. *The Great Midwest Flood.* New York: Little, Brown (1995).

Read More

Calhoun, Mary. *Flood.* New York: HarperCollins (1997).

Kalz, Jill. *Floods.* North Mankato, MN: Smart Apple Media (2002).

Thompson, Luke. *Floods.* Danbury, CT: Children's Press (2000).

Learn More Online

Visit these Web sites to learn more about floods:

- www.fema.gov/kids/floods.htm
- www.noaa.gov/floods.html
- www.redcross.org/services/disaster/0,1082,0_585_,00. html

Index

dam
12–13, 14–15

Des Moines, Iowa
9, 28

disaster kit
26

flash flood
12–13, 14–15, 28–29

flood barriers
24–25, 29

floodplains
22–23, 29

Florida
8

Galveston, Texas
28

Grafton, Illinois
28

Halstead, Kansas
5

Illinois
5, 6–7, 16, 22–23

Iowa
7, 9

Johnstown, Pennsylvania
14–15

Kansas
7

levees
13, 16–17, 21, 29

map
7

Midwest
6–7, 8, 11, 17, 18, 23, 28

Minnesota
7, 10

Mississippi River
11, 13, 23

Missouri
4, 7, 20, 23, 27

Missouri River
4, 11, 23

Nebraska
7

New Orleans, Louisiana
29

North Dakota
7

sandbags
17, 24

shelter
5

South Dakota
7, 29

United States (U.S.)
11, 12, 14, 28

Valmeyer, Illinois
22–23

volunteers
17

wetlands
20–21, 23

Wisconsin
7

About the Author

Barbara Knox lives with her daughter, Annie, near the Mississippi River in Minnesota. She saw the floodwaters spread into St. Paul, Minnesota, in the summer of 1993.